ANGEL ISLAND IMMIGRATION

A HISTORY PERSPECTIVES BOOK

Jamie Kallio

Published in the United States of America
by Cherry Lake Publishing
Ann Arbor, Michigan
www.cherrylakepublishing.com

Consultants: Carl L. Bankston III, Professor, Sociology Department & Asian Studies
Program, Tulane University; Marla Conn, ReadAbility, Inc.
Editorial direction: Red Line Editorial
Book design: Sleeping Bear Press

Photo Credits: Library of Congress, cover (left), cover (middle), cover (right), 1 (left),
1 (middle), 1 (right), 14, 24; Bettmann/Corbis, 4; J. D. Givens/Library of Congress, 7;
The U.S. National Archives and Records Administration, 8; Carol M. Highsmith/
Library of Congress, 11; AP Images, 17, 30; Corbis, 19; Kirn Vintage Stock/Corbis, 22;
Arnold Genthe/Library of Congress, 27; Robert Galbraith/Reuters/Corbis, 28

Library of Congress Cataloging-in-Publication Data
Kallio, Jamie.
  Angel Island immigration / Jamie Kallio.
    pages cm. -- (Perspectives library)
  Includes bibliographical references and index.
  ISBN 978-1-63137-614-6 (hardcover) -- ISBN 978-1-63137-659-7 (pbk.) -- ISBN
978-1-63137-704-4 (pdf ebook) -- ISBN 978-1-63137-749-5 (hosted ebook)
1. Angel Island (Calif.)--History--Juvenile literature. 2. Chinese Americans--History--
20th century--Juvenile literature. 3. United States--Emigration and immigration--
History--20th century--Juvenile literature. 4. China--Emigration and immigration--
History--20th century--Juvenile literature. I. Title.
F868.S156K35 2014
979.462--dc23

                              2014004580

Cherry Lake Publishing would like to acknowledge the work of
The Partnership for 21st Century Skills. Please visit *www.p21.org*
for more information.

Printed in the United States of America
Corporate Graphics Inc.
July 2014

TABLE OF CONTENTS

In this book, you will read about Angel Island immigration from three perspectives. Each perspective is based on real things that happened to real people who lived during the years of immigration through Angel Island, from 1910 to 1940. As you'll see, the same event can look different depending on one's point of view.

1

Chew Hoy Fong

Paper Son

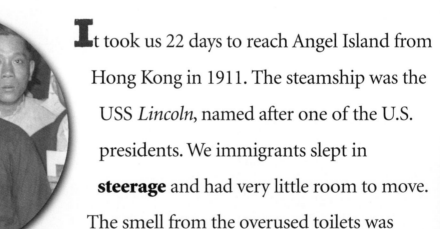

It took us 22 days to reach Angel Island from Hong Kong in 1911. The steamship was the USS *Lincoln*, named after one of the U.S. presidents. We immigrants slept in **steerage** and had very little room to move. The smell from the overused toilets was horrible. Many people were seasick. Luckily, I did not mind the rocking of the ship too much. Thoughts of the past and the future kept my mind busy.

When we came into San Francisco Bay, I knew for the first time how far I was from my village back in Guangdong. I remembered the last time I saw my family: Ma and Ba, Amah, my three younger sisters, and my baby brother, standing in front of the house waving goodbye. I am the eldest—18 years old. After the last flood ruined our crops, something had to be done. It was decided I would go to *gam saan* (gold mountain).

Ba had to sell some of his farmland to raise money for the trip. Ma and Amah sold embroidery to help. Ba even borrowed money from Uncle, who is cheap and mean (though I would never say this to Ba). We had to pay not only my passage but also a special fee to my paper father in the United States. My paper father is not related to me. He is the cousin of our neighbor. He agreed to pretend to be my father so I might get into the United States. Those who pay someone in the United States like this are called paper sons. Chinese are not allowed into the country anymore unless they are in a special class, which includes merchants and students. My paper father owns a shop, so he is allowed to **vouch** for me. I do not like lying, but this is the only way I can enter the country. The Chinese government has taxed farmers too much. With the droughts of last year and the floods this spring, the crops have done poorly. There is barely enough rice to feed us all.

I will make my fortune in gam saan and send it home. I will repay our debts and my family will be rich. My sisters and baby brother will never go to sleep hungry again. But first I must pass my hearing, a meeting where I will be asked many questions before I can enter the country.

The Angel Island station is on top of a hill. It is a wooden house

THINK ABOUT IT

▶ Determine the main point of this paragraph. Pick out one piece of evidence that supports it.

▲ *The Angel Island station was the first stop for many immigrants landing on the West Coast of the United States.*

with a yard fenced in by barbed wire. The others tell me that at the old station the Chinese would escape through the windows and hide in San Francisco, never to be seen again. The fence and U.S. guards in this station keep us from running off. To me it looks like a cage.

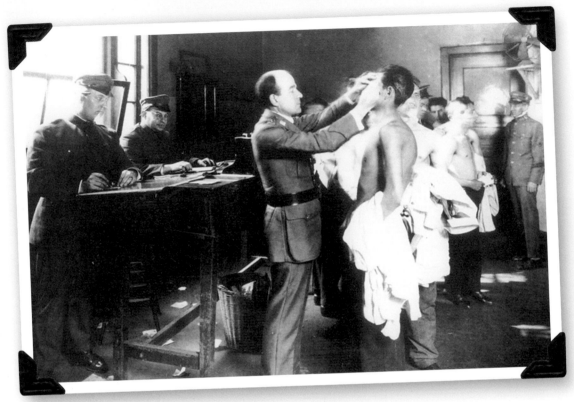

▲ *Health inspectors examined new immigrants for diseases or other health problems.*

I have passed the medical exam. We had to strip and were poked by an angry-faced white man. He checked our teeth and eyes. Then a nurse handed each of us a small basin. I did not know what to do with it. The man next to me said we must relieve ourselves in the basin so they can test our stool. The doctors check for worms and diseases. If someone has worms, he is **deported**. I am not very worried, since I know I am healthy. But others are not so lucky. They had liver fluke or hookworm and were denied entrance to gam saan.

I have waited inside the station almost three weeks for my hearing. I do not know why it takes so long. In that time, I have felt both nervous and excited. There is not much to do. Some who have been here several months have record players. Others get newspapers from the kitchen help, who are all Chinese. The white guards let us outside every morning for an hour. The guards do not like us. I cannot understand what they say, but it is plain in their hard eyes and tight mouths that they think less of us. The first time I was allowed outside, I had to squint because the sun was so bright. I stood by the barbed wire and looked out over the bay, across to San Francisco. I imagine my new life there. I am not afraid to work hard. My paper father has promised that he will help me find a job.

The food is disgusting. The cooks throw chunks of pork and shredded vegetables all together in a soup pot. I can hardly swallow it, but I force myself because I must stay strong. There is a sign on the wall in Cantonese that warns us not to throw food. If one has money, there is a small store in the dining hall where crackers and peanuts can be bought. I do not have extra money though.

Most of the time I sit idle and think through the information my paper father sent in his coaching book. These are special books written by paper fathers and sent to those of us immigrating to the

SECOND SOURCE

▶ Find a second source about paper sons. Compare the information there to the information in this source.

▲ *Many of the poems written on the walls of Angel Island still exist.*

United States. Inside the books are things about our paper fathers' villages and families that we must memorize. We do this because the questions asked at the hearings are very hard. I have memorized my paper father's name, the names of his father and mother, and the names of his grandparents, brothers, and cousins. The **interrogator** cannot possibly ask me more than that. My paper father has described the way his house looked in the village where he grew up. He told me about the chickens and water buffalo his family owned. He even told me the names of the neighbors on either side of the house, just in case. We have all heard how hard the hearings can be. The interrogators ask many, many questions, waiting for you to make a mistake. But I will not make a mistake. I threw my coaching book into the ocean before we came into the harbor. If officials catch us with the books, we will be sent home.

All I can do now is wait. Others who have been **detained** have written on the walls. Some words have been scrawled with pencil. Others have been carved into the wood. They are from men like me, waiting for a better life in gam saan. They are from those who were deported back to China, which is a great shame. The guards lock us in and turn out the lights at nine o'clock at night. Last night, before it got dark,

I took a pencil and wrote my own words on a wall:

> *This may be hardship*
>
> *But we have known worse*
>
> *I endure*
>
> *And imagine the waves sweeping me out*
>
> *To where my fortune lies*

GOLD MOUNTAIN

In 1848, gold was discovered in California's mountains. Cantonese merchants spread the news in China. They called California and then other western U.S. states the "gold mountain" because of this gold. Chinese people wanted to come to gold mountain because of the hardships they suffered at home.

Fei Yen Lee

Chinese Immigrant Wife

I feel much despair. My husband in the United States wants me and our children to join him. We made preparations to travel from China. He sent the money for our passage. I carefully packed bags for myself and our children. Our families in the village had a party for us to say goodbye. My mind was at ease. I thought there would be no trouble because we have no reason to lie to get into the United States. My husband is a tea merchant. He has been **naturalized**. He is a U.S. citizen living an honest life in San Francisco.

I was very ill on the steamship here. I could not keep much food in my stomach, so now I am very thin. The baby fretted the whole trip as well. Mai Lin and Sue Li behaved well, even though our traveling quarters were cramped and dirty.

When the ship came into the harbor at San Francisco Bay, I thought our long journey was finally over. White guards greeted us with stern faces and hard eyes. First they took us by ferry, a smaller boat, to the dock of Angel Island. Then they made us leave all our bags behind in a small building. Sue Li cried because her little toy dog was in her bag. The guards

ANALYZE THIS

▶ Analyze both Chew Hoy's and Fei Yen's experiences at Angel Island. How are they different? In what ways are they similar?

would not allow her to take it with her. I wonder why we even bothered to pack.

The men and women were separated to different dormitories. All children under the age of 12 were allowed to stay with their mothers. This is a good thing, since Sue Li won't let me out of her sight. They have split up the husbands and wives who came here together. They are not allowed to visit one another. Next we had medical examinations. This was worse than being seasick. It was terrible to undress in front of complete strangers! All the Chinese women I know are modest. I felt very embarrassed during my medical exam, but the children and I passed.

There are women here who guard us, called matrons. They are very tall and wear long, heavy skirts with puffy blouses. They watch over us and lock us in our dormitory at night. The matrons are not very kind, but there is another woman who visits all the time. She is a deaconess, a religious woman, who comes from the

▲ *Chinese and Japanese women and children waited to be processed in an area surrounded by wire mesh at Angel Island.*

Women's Home **Missionary** Society. Her name is Eugenia, but she has told us to call her Jean. Jean is very kind to all the Chinese women here and especially to the children. She teaches us English and has brought small toys for the children.

The women are glad for Jean's visits. If not for her, we would cry from boredom. Many of us have been waiting in this station for two, three, and even four weeks. The men detained here have a special group called *Zizhihiu*. They have officers who guide the group. They also raise money for books and music. I can read, but most Chinese women do not receive education. For this reason the women do not have a group, and we have very little to amuse

ZIZHIHIU

The *Zizhihiu*, or the Angel Island Liberty Association, was a group created by the male detainees at Angel Island. They helped each other and collected dues from other members. With that money they bought things to help pass the time, such as books, newspapers, and record players.

ourselves. The days are so long. Sometimes we are allowed outside with the matrons to be in the sun and fresh air. I have come to hate the sight of the barbed wire fence. We are prisoners here, plain and simple.

▲ *Immigration officials sometimes questioned and examined immigrants aboard the ships they arrived on.*

My hearing happened two weeks into our detention here. I thought all I had to do was tell the truth and the officials would allow me to join my husband. After so long apart, we were finally to be together as a whole family. But I have somehow failed the **interrogation**. The girls and I are supposed to be deported back to China.

The officials say I made too many mistakes during my hearing. They say I did not answer all the questions correctly, and so I must be lying. They questioned my daughters separately from me. They say the girls answered a great many of the questions wrong.

As for the questions they asked me, I find them ridiculous. I can answer things about my husband's family and mother-in-law's house,

SECOND SOURCE

▶ Find a second source that describes Chinese wives coming to the United States through Angel Island. Compare the information there to the information in this source.

where I lived for so long. But how am I to know where the rice bin is kept in the house of the neighbor three doors down?

I blame the paper sons. There are so many of them trying to get into America illegally. This makes it harder for the rest of us, because now the whites think we are all liars. I am the wife of a Chinese merchant. My children are the daughters of a Chinese merchant. We have not lied. The liars should be the ones going back to China, not us.

Jean tries to cheer me. She tells me not to give up hope. She has written to the Department of Commerce and Labor on my behalf. All we can do now is wait—and hope.

Deaconess Eugenia "Jean" Anderson

Missionary

I believe in helping the unfortunate, but sometimes being a missionary is hard. There are so many Chinese women with young children waiting here at Angel Island. Most are terrified, for they do not speak English. They do not understand our ways. All they want to do is join their husbands who are either living separately in the men's barracks here at the station or are already established in San Francisco. Can you imagine your family being broken up across an ocean for years? Some of the children have only met their fathers once or twice. Their despair is something I can almost touch.

There is not much in the detention hall to amuse the women and children. Even when we supply books, many cannot read. I am trying to fix that by giving English lessons to all who are interested. I hope to prepare them for their hearings and the time when they are allowed into the country.

I have friends who do not understand my work with the Chinese. My brother-in-law has been out of work for quite some time. He blames this on Chinese men. The Chinese

SECOND SOURCE

▶ Find a second source that describes how U.S. workers viewed Chinese people entering the country. Compare the information there to the information in this source.

are hard-working people, and they will take the worst jobs at very little pay. My brother-in-law says they are stealing work from him and other Americans. I do not agree, but it's hard to argue with him. Many others have the same opinion.

▲ An 1880 newspaper illustration shows the stereotype that Chinese men were taking the jobs that women once did, leaving the women with nothing to do.

I admit that the Chinese take some getting used to. They dress differently from Americans. Their language is odd. The men wear their hair in long braids down their backs. Their native food is strange and so are their customs. They even have different gods. There are some in authority who feel they can never **assimilate** into our culture. But aside from all this, they are still people. They deserve our kindness and generosity.

I find the interrogators here to be very harsh at times. They are not quite as hard on immigrants who are not Asian. One of the guards told me that all the Chinese are trying to get into the country by illegal means. This is why the questions at the hearings are so hard. The interrogators want to flush out any lies. After the earthquake and fire of 1906, San Francisco's Hall of Records was destroyed. All the records of births, marriages, and deaths are gone. There is no way to check if a Chinese immigrant is

EXCLUSION ACT OF 1882

The Chinese Exclusion Act of 1882 stopped most Chinese immigration into the United States for ten years. Only Chinese teachers, students, officials, and merchants were allowed into the country. All other Chinese immigrants were unable to apply for citizenship. The act was renewed in 1892 and 1902. It was made permanent in 1904. The act was not reversed until 1943.

trying to enter the country illegally or not. Since the records are destroyed, there is no way to prove if an immigrant is married to someone in the city.

As a result, many of the detainees are turned away and sent back home. The Chinese interpreter told me of the troubles in China. The government is falling apart. Bad weather has damaged crops. Many people

▲ *Much of San Francisco sat in ruins after the 1906 earthquake.*

are starving. If my homeland was in such a poor state, I would also seek refuge in another country.

The conditions here can be quite depressing as well. The men in the Angel Island Liberty Association have filed complaints for more soap and toilet paper. The women's dormitory is small, with bunks stacked in threes upon each other. Towels and clothing hang from lines stretched between bunks. The meals are

▲ *Visitors can now see the barracks where Chinese and Japanese immigrants were once held at Angel Island.*

not well prepared. This is because the authorities buy food from the cheapest suppliers. Many of the women refuse to eat at mealtimes. The children do not seem to care, for they eat everything set before them.

I bring donations of clothes, toys, wool, and knitting needles. This helps the detainees pass the time.

Often I will take a family under my wing. There is a mother here named Fei Yen who is very distraught. She has three small girls with her. Her husband has been living in the United States for many years. It is only now that he can afford to have all of them together. Yet Fei Yen failed her hearing. She is due to be deported. There is no reason why Fei Yen and her girls should be denied. They have the right papers. Her husband has paid for a lawyer to appeal the ruling. I feel the Chinese Exclusion Act has set a dangerous example. If we **discriminate** against entire ethnic groups, what will happen to us in the future?

THINK ABOUT IT

▶ Determine the main point of this chapter. Pick out a sentence or paragraph that supports it.

LOOK, LOOK AGAIN

This image shows a Chinese man being questioned at Angel Island. Use this photograph to answer the following questions:

1. How would a paper son hoping to be allowed into the United States react to this photo? What might he say about the interrogation process?

2. How do you think a Chinese woman traveling with children would describe this photo? What might she tell her family in China about this photo?

3. What would a missionary woman notice about this scene? How would she describe the hearing to other missionary women?

GLOSSARY

assimilate (uh-SI-muh-late) to adopt the ways of a different society or country

deport (di-PORT) to force a person who is not a citizen to leave a country

detain (di-TAYN) to hold or keep someone back when he or she wants to go somewhere

discriminate (diss-KRIM-uh-nate) to treat a person or group of people unfairly

interrogation (in-TER-uh-gay-shun) asking someone questions in a detailed way

interrogator (in-TER-uh-gay-ter) someone who asks detailed questions at a formal meeting

missionary (MISH-uh-ner-ee) a person who is sent to teach about religion and do religious work

naturalize (NACH-ur-uh-lize) to grant citizenship to a person who was born in a different country

steerage (STEER-ij) the part of a ship where the cheapest cabins are located

vouch (VAUCH) to guarantee that someone or something is honest or good

LEARN MORE

Further Reading

Brimner, Larry Dane. *Angel Island*. New York: Children's Press, 2001.
Flanagan, Alice K. *Angel Island*. Minneapolis: Compass Point Books, 2006.
Freedman, Russell. *Angel Island: Gateway to Gold Mountain*. New York: Clarion Books, 2013.

Web Sites

Angel Island Immigration Station Foundation
http://www.aiisf.org
This is the official Web site of Angel Island Immigration Station and includes information on its history and interviews with detainees.

Discovering Angel Island: The Story Behind the Poems
http://www.kqed.org/w/pacificlink/history/angelisland/video/
This Web site contains a video showing and discussing the poems written on the walls of the barracks at Angel Island.

INDEX

ABOUT THE AUTHOR

Jamie Kallio is a youth services librarian in the south suburbs of Chicago. She has a master's degree in writing for children and young adults from Hamline University in Minnesota. History is one of her passions, along with flavored coffee and episodes of *Doctor Who*. She lives with her husband and a house full of lively pets.